EARNING, SAVING, SPENDING

Credit Cards and Checks

Margaret Hall

Heinemann Library
Chicago, Illinois

©2008 Heinemann Library
a division of Reed Elsevier Inc.
Chicago, Illinois

Customer Service 888-454-2279
Visit our website at www.heinemannlibrary.com

Designed by Kimberly R. Miracle and Cavedweller Studio
Photo research by Tracy Cummins and Heather Mauldin
Illustrations by Mark Preston Illustration
Printed by Leo Printing Company

12 11 10 09 08
10 9 8 7 6 5 4 3 2 1

New edition ISBNS: 978-1-4034-9816-8 (hardcover)
                    978-1-4034-9821-2 (paperback)

Library of Congress Cataloging-in-Publication Data
Hall, Margaret, 1947-
  Credit cards and checks / Margaret Hall. -- 2nd ed.
     p. cm. -- (Earning, saving, spending)
  Includes bibliographical references and index.
  Summary: This text gives students an overview of spending money without
using cash, including details on credit, checkbooks, debt and interest.
  ISBN 978-1-4034-9816-8 (hc) -- ISBN 978-1-4034-9821-2 (pb)
  1. Checks--Juvenile literature. 2. Credit cards--Juvenile literature. 3.
Debit cards--Juvenile literature. I. Title.
  HG1691.H32 2008
  332.76--dc22

                         2007015150

Acknowledgments
The author and publishers are grateful to the following for permission to reproduce copyright
material: Alamy **pp. 22** (Jack Sparticus), **23** (eStock Photo); Getty Images **pp. 4** (Gary Buss), **6**
(Bruce Ayres), **17** (PM Images), **24** (Kevin Hatt), **26** (Bill Losh), **27** (PM Images), **28** (PBJ Pictures),
29 (Eri Morita); PhotoEdit **pp. 7** (Michael Newman), **14** (David Young-Wolff), **18** (Spencer Grant), **21**
(Robert W. Ginn); Redux **p. 15** (Jason Kempin); Shutterstock **p. 19.**

Cover photographs reproduced with permission of Royalty free/Corbis and Royalty free/ Getty
Images (piggybank).

Every effort has been made to contact copyright holders of any material reproduced in this book.
Any omissions will be rectified in subsequent printings if notice is given to the publisher.

Disclaimer
All the Internet addresses (URLs) given in this book were valid at the time of going to press.
However, due to the dynamic nature of the Internet, some addresses may have changed, or sites
may have changed or ceased to exist since publication. While the author and publisher regret any
inconvenience this may cause readers, no responsibility for any such changes can be accepted by
either the author or the publisher.

Contents

Some words are shown in bold, **like this**. You can find out what they mean by looking in the glossary.

Spending Without Cash

Banks offer services to their customers that let them buy things without using **cash**. These services include **checks** and special **bank cards**. A check is like a note telling the bank to pay money to someone. Bank cards are thin, plastic cards. Both can be used in many places.

Most stores let customers use checks and bank cards to buy items.

In some ways, it is safer to use checks or bank cards to buy things. If cash gets lost or stolen, anyone can use it. Checks and bank cards have the owner's name on them. Only that person can easily use them. People usually have to prove that a check or bank card belongs to them before they can use it.

A person often has to show identification when using a check or bank card, for extra safety.

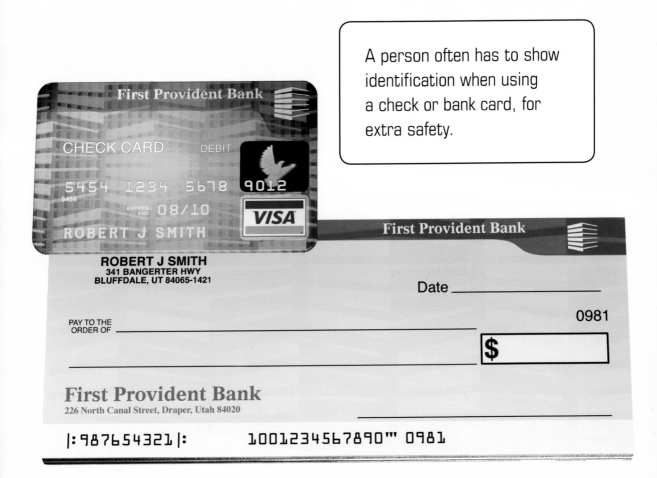

Opening a Checking Account

One way to pay for things without **cash** is by using a **check**. To do this, a person must have a **checking account**. To open a checking account, the customer gives the bank some money. This is called a **deposit**.

Banks offer different types of checking accounts.

When a person opens a checking account, the bank gives him or her a **checkbook** with a check register.

The checks can be used like cash. Every time the person uses a check or makes a deposit, he or she should record the information in the **check register**. That way, the person will always know how much money is in the account.

Paying by Check

Checks have information printed on them. The account owner's name and address are printed in one corner, and the number of the check is printed in another corner. There is also an **account number** that tells the bank who owns the **checking account**.

This is what a check looks like.

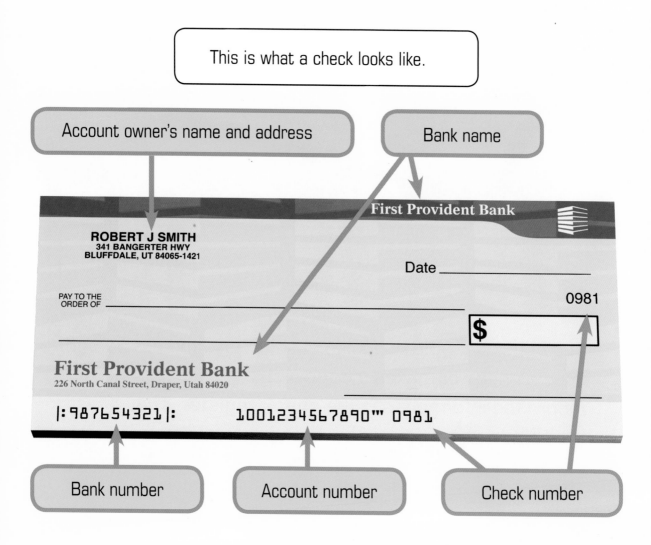

Account owner's name and address

Bank name

ROBERT J SMITH
341 BANGERTER HWY
BLUFFDALE, UT 84065-1421

Date _____

PAY TO THE
ORDER OF _____

0981

$

First Provident Bank

First Provident Bank
226 North Canal Street, Draper, Utah 84020

|: 987654321 |:   1001234567890''' 0981

Bank number

Account number

Check number

A person has to fill in a check with certain information before it can be used to pay for something.

Person or company being paid

Date

First Provident Bank

ROBERT J SMITH
341 BANGERTER HWY
BLUFFDALE, UT 84065-1421

Date MARCH 15, 2008

PAY TO THE
ORDER OF _STEPHEN BRAND._

0981

ONE HUNDRED DOLLARS AND 00/100 $100 — 00

First Provident Bank
226 North Canal Street, Draper, Utah 84020

Robert J Smith

|:987654321|:   1001234567890'" 0981

Amount written in numbers and in words

Signature

To use a check to pay for something, a person must fill in the date, whom is to be paid, and how much the bank should pay them. The account owner also has to put his or her signature at the bottom of the check.

What Happens to a Check?

Do you know what happens to a **check** after it is written? Here is the story of one check.

1. Robert writes a check for $50 to pay for dog food.

2. The store sends the check to its bank.

3. The bank sends the check to the **clearinghouse** that keeps track of its business.

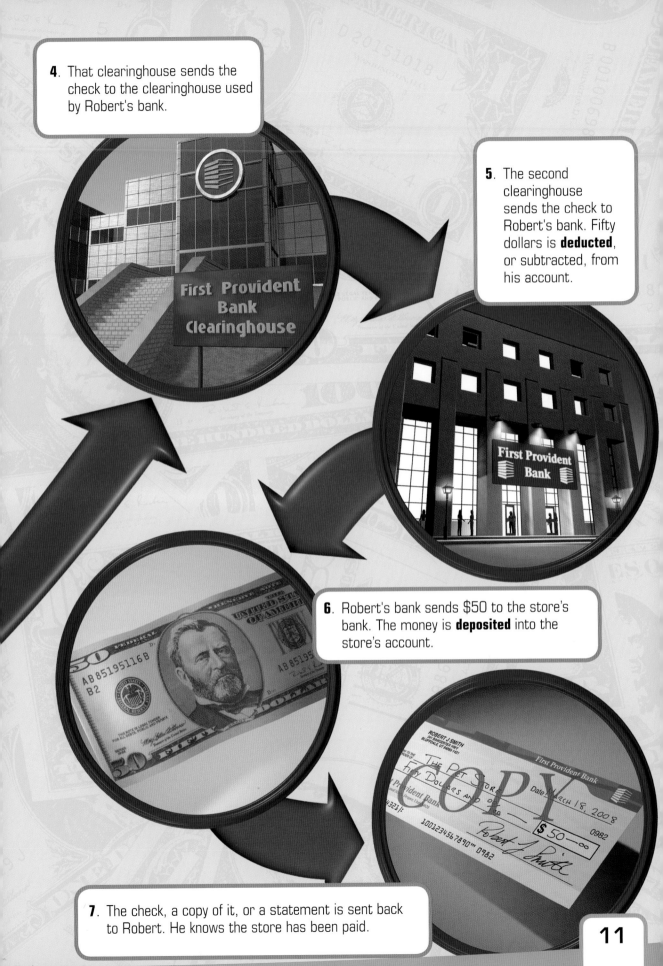

4. That clearinghouse sends the check to the clearinghouse used by Robert's bank.

5. The second clearinghouse sends the check to Robert's bank. Fifty dollars is **deducted**, or subtracted, from his account.

First Provident Bank Clearinghouse

First Provident Bank

6. Robert's bank sends $50 to the store's bank. The money is **deposited** into the store's account.

7. The check, a copy of it, or a statement is sent back to Robert. He knows the store has been paid.

Debit Cards

People can use the money in their **checking accounts** without writing checks. They do this with a **debit card**. The numbers on the front of the card tell the bank what **account number** the card goes with. The card also has the account owner's name printed on the front. The owner must also put his or her signature on the back of the card.

Debit cards have the owner's signature on them and numbers that tell the bank who owns the account.

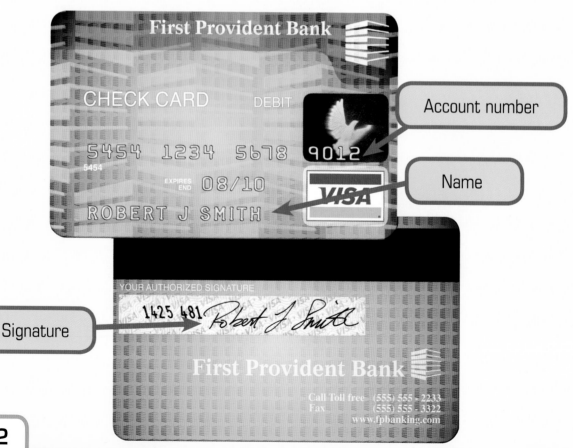

Account number

Name

Signature

First Provident Bank

Check Register

Check Number	Date	Transaction Description	Amount	Fee	Deposit	Balance
	02/08	BALANCE FORWARD				1503.76
ATM	02/09	CASH	100.00			1403.76
979	02/10	BIG SOUNDS MUSIC	63.20			1340.58
CARD	02/15	GAS STATION	27.50			1313.08
	02/20	MARK LOAN REPAYMENT			350.00	1663.08
	02/23	SUPERMARKET	93.15			1569.93
980	02/28	RENT	1020.25			549.68
	03/02	PAY CHECK			812.14	1361.82
981	03/15	STEVES HI FI SHACK	100.00			1261.82
ATM	03/16	CASH	20.00			1241.82

Member of the FDIC
Call Toll free   (555) 555 - 2233
Fax   (555) 555 - 3322
www.fpbanking.com

226 North Canal Street, Draper, Utah 84020

Debit card owners must keep track of their checking accounts so they do not spend more money than what they really have.

When people use debit cards, the money comes from their checking accounts. Card owners must have enough money in their checking accounts to pay for what they buy. A card owner should record debit card purchases in his or her **check register**. This will help the person keep track of how much money is in the account.

How Debit Cards Work

Every **debit card** has a magnetic strip on the back. The strip has a code in it that gives the **account number**. A person puts the debit card through a special machine at a store. This machine is hooked up to the bank's computers. It reads the code and **deducts** the money from the person's **checking account**. The bank's computers send the money to the store's bank account.

High-speed computers let stores and businesses check a customer's account information almost instantly.

Businesses must pay banks a **fee** every time a customer uses a debit or **credit card** to pay for a purchase.

Usually, a person has to enter a **personal identification number (PIN)** into the debit card machine. Only the account owner should know the PIN. Sometimes the customer must sign a **receipt** that the store will keep. The person will get a copy of the receipt that shows how much he or she spent.

Checking a Checkbook

Every month, the bank makes a **bank statement** for each customer. It shows everything that happened with the person's accounts that month. It lists all the checks that came back to the bank to be paid. It also lists purchases made with a **debit card**. Checks and debit card purchases are **deducted** from the person's **checking account**.

First Provident Bank
226 North Canal Street, Draper, Utah 84020

Account owner's name

Beginning and ending date for statement

Checking account number

Beginning total

Money left in account

Withdrawal

Deposit

Check payment

ROBERT J SMITH
341 BANGERTER HWY
BLUFFDALE UT 84065-1421

MONTHLY CLIENT UPDATE
Statement Date: 04/03/08
Page 1 of 2
Account Number   12345678

CHECKING STATEMENT

Statement Cycle:	30 days
Begining Balance:	1503.76
Deposits/ Misc Credits:	1162.14
Withdrawals/Misc Debits:	1304.10
Ending Balance:	1361.82

Service Charge: .0
Average Balance: 1298.4
Enclosures:

TRANSACTION DETAILS

Date	Description	Withdrawals	Deposits	Balance
02/09/08	ATM WITHDRAWAL/TRANS 12345	100.00		1340.58
02/10/08	CHECK PAID #979	63.20		1313.08
02/15/08	POS PURCHASE CHECK/TRANS	27.50		1663.08
			350.00	1569.93
02/20/08	DDA DEPOSIT			549.68
02/23/08	POS PUR/PIN CHK/TRANS 12345	93.15		
02/28/08	CHECK PAID # 980	1020.25		
03/02/08	CASH DEPOSIT		812.14	

1001.50

CHECKS POSTED

Date	Check No.	Amount
02/10/08	0979	63.20
02/28/08	0980	1020.25

ATM-DEBIT CARD SUMMARY

Date	Type	Amount	Location
			ATM WITHDRAWAL, BLUFFDALE UT

Bank statements help customers keep track of their money.

The statement shows every **deposit** made to the checking account, too. These are added to the account. The statement shows how much money is still in the checking account. It is important to look over a bank statement carefully to be sure that there are no mistakes.

The amount of money in a person's bank statement and **check register** should match.

Buy Now and Pay Later

People can buy things without using **cash**, **checks**, or **debit cards**. They can buy things even when they do not have the money to pay for them right away. Buying things this way is called buying on **credit**. It is like getting a **loan**. The money has to be paid back later.

To get a **credit card** or loan, a person must have a record showing that he or she pays **bills** on time.

Banks and credit card companies offer different kinds of credit cards to customers.

To buy things on credit, people use another special card called a credit card. Every credit card has a **credit limit**. This is the greatest amount of money a person can spend using the card. The person has to pay some money to the credit card company every month to be allowed to keep using the card.

Credit Cards

Many banks give **credit cards** to their customers. There are also credit card companies, stores, and other businesses that offer cards. A credit card looks like a **debit card**. On the front it has the name of the bank or credit card company, a special **account number**, and the customer's name. On the back, it has a magnetic strip and the account owner's signature.

Credit cards and debit cards have a **security code** inside the signature box, often used to make **online** purchases.

First Provident Bank

5454 1234 5678 9012
5454
EXPIRES END 08/10
VISA
ROBERT J SMITH

Account number

YOUR AUTHORIZED SIGNATURE
2734 762 Robert J Smith
First Provident Bank

Call Toll free (555) 555 - 2233
Fax (555) 555 - 3322
www.fpbanking.com

Magnetic strip

Signature

Security code

If a debit or credit card gets lost or stolen, the bank or credit card company must be told right away. That way, the card can be canceled so no one else can use it. It is important to keep track of **bank cards**.

Card owners must report lost credit cards to the bank or credit card company right away.

How Credit Cards Work

Like a **debit card**, a **credit card** goes through a special machine. The machine reads the code on the back of the card and prints out a **receipt**. The credit card owner signs the receipt and the store clerk checks the **signature**.

The signature on the receipt must match the signature on the card. If it does not, the store clerk will not complete the sale.

Some stores keep customers' signatures on file in their computer instead of keeping signed receipts.

Some stores do not make customers sign paper receipts. Instead, a person signs his or her name on a small computer screen using a special pen. Either way, the customer gets a receipt for his or her records. Once every month, the credit card owner gets a **bill**. The bill lists all the purchases made with the credit card. The owner should check the bill carefully.

Interest

A **credit card** owner can pay the whole **bill** at once or just part of it. The amount paid right away is the payment. The amount left over is the **balance**. The balance is a **loan**.

This woman is writing a **check** to pay her credit card bill.

FIRST CARD

Visa® Statement

Transactions (continued)

Date	Description
Aug 23	Uncle Dan's Ltd
Aug 25	Northside Cat...
Aug 26	

Account number

Visa® Statement

Closing Date August 27, 2009
Account 4673-891-456-543

Payment due now

Minimum payment due **$22.00**
Payment Due Date . . . . September 2...

Account summary

Previous Balance	**$1,675.89**
Payments and credits	
Transactions	
Finance charges (due to periodic rate)	**10.26**
New Balance	$1,090.46

Total credit line $15,000

Finance charge
$10.26

$10.26

Mileage Plus miles earned with First Card

Miles earned this month from purchases 1,080

Interest charged **Balance from last month**

Trans...

Date						
Jul 30		Chicago	IL	V		$39.42
Aug 1	J. Crew	800-9320043	VA	V		63.92
Aug 2	Matsuya Restaurant	Chicago	IL	V		56.12
Aug 3	Original Levi's Str 108	Chicago	IL	V		67.43
Aug 6	The North Face 010	Chicago	IL	V		

> Credit card owners need to check their bills carefully. They should not spend more than they will be able to pay back.

The bank or credit card company lets the account owner borrow the money, but it charges a **fee** for this service. This fee is called **interest**, and it is added to the person's next bill. The longer it takes to pay a bill completely, the more interest the person will end up paying. So it is smart to pay the total amount of the bill as quickly as possible.

Debt

A **debt** is money owed to someone. A **credit card balance** is a kind of debt. There are other types of debts. Most people do not have enough money to pay for a house, car, or college education all at once. They borrow money from a bank or **loan** company.

Many people use loans to help pay for college. They will pay back the loans after college, when they have jobs.

This man is checking to see how much interest he owes.

Like any other debt, credit card debt must be paid back. The money does not have to be paid all at once. However, **interest** is added to the amount owed. The longer it takes to pay, the more interest is charged. Interest adds up quickly. It makes debts harder to pay back. So it is important to use credit cards wisely.

Using Credit Wisely

One way to use **credit** wisely is to not use it too often. Another is to pay **credit card debts** quickly. Everyone has certain needs. Food, clothing, transportation, and a place to live are all examples of things people must buy.

Families usually spend much of their money on food.

Wants are things like vacations, fancy cars, restaurant meals, or even expensive makeup.

Everyone also has wants. These are things people can get along without, but might like to have or do. People should think carefully about what they buy so they do not go into debt for things they do not really need. It is important to make wise choices about how to spend money.

Glossary

account number number that tells to whom a bank account belongs

balance amount of money still owed

bank card plastic card given by a bank to a customer that can be used to buy things without using cash

bank statement record of what happens to the money a person keeps in the bank

bill record that shows how much someone owes at a certain time

cash coins and paper money

check note from the owner of a checking account telling the bank to pay money from the account to someone

checkbook booklet of checks

check register booklet for keeping track of how checks are used

checking account service offered by a bank that lets people use money without carrying cash

clearinghouse business that helps a bank take care of its money

credit borrowed money

credit card thin, plastic bank card that lets someone buy something and pay for it later

credit limit total amount of money a person can borrow

debit card bank card that lets someone pay for something using money in his or her checking account

debt money owed to someone else

deduct to take away or subtract

deposit to put money into a bank account

fee money charged for a service

interest fee charged for borrowing money; or money paid to people for letting the bank use their money to run its business

loan money someone borrows

online connected to the Internet, which is a network of computers around the world through which information is shared

payment amount of a bill that is paid at one time

personal identification number (PIN) secret number only the account owner knows and uses at ATMs and debit card machines to deposit and withdraw money from accounts

receipt record of how much something cost or how much a person spent

security code numbers found inside the signature box of bank cards that are used as an extra safety measure for **online** purchases

Find Out More

Basel, Roberta. *Checks, Credit, and Debit Cards.* Bloomington, MN: Capstone Press, 2006.

Bailey, Gerry and Felicia Law. *Cowries, Coins, Credit: The History of Money.* Bloomington, MN: Compass Point Books, 2006.

Stone, L. *Paying by Credit.* Vero Beach, FL: Rourke Publishing, 2003.

To learn more about money in the United States, visit the United States Department of the Treasury Education website at: http://www.ustreas.gov/education/

Index